Great White Sharks

by Nico Barnes

ABDO
SHARKS
Kids

Visit us at www.abdopublishing.com

Published by Abdo Kids, a division of ABDO, PO Box 398166, Minneapolis, Minnesota 55439.

Copyright © 2015 by Abdo Consulting Group, Inc. International copyrights reserved in all countries.
No part of this book may be reproduced in any form without written permission from the publisher.

Printed in the United States of America, North Mankato, Minnesota.

032014

092014

PRINTED ON RECYCLED PAPER

Photo Credits: iStock, Thinkstock

Production Contributors: Teddy Borth, Jennie Forsberg, Grace Hansen

Design Contributors: Dorothy Toth, Renée LaViolette, Laura Rask

Library of Congress Control Number: 2013952570

Cataloging-in-Publication Data

Barnes, Nico.

 Great white sharks / Nico Barnes.

   p. cm. -- (Sharks)

ISBN 978-1-62970-065-6 (lib. bdg.)

Includes bibliographical references and index.

1. White sharks--Juvenile literature.   I. Title.

597.3--dc23

                    2013952570

Table of Contents

Great White Sharks

The great white shark is one
of the biggest fish in the sea.

Great white sharks live in ocean waters around the world. They like **mild** temperatures.

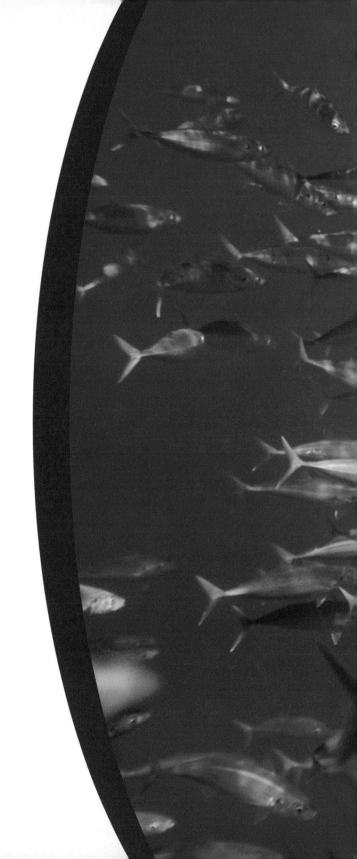

7

Great white sharks have
grayish upper bodies.
They get their name for
their white underbellies.

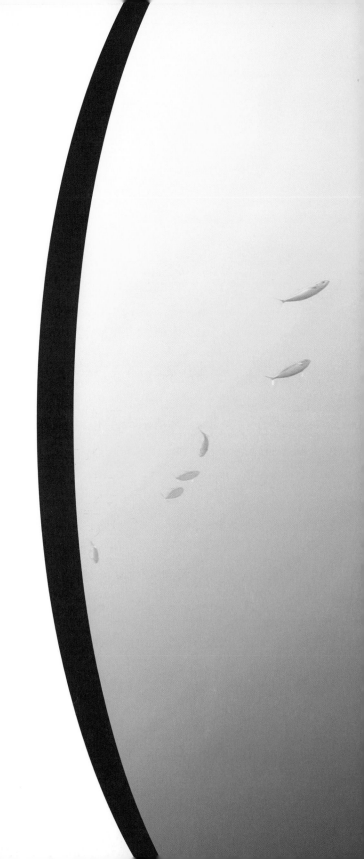

Great white sharks look like torpedoes. They have strong tails. They are built to swim fast!

Great white sharks cannot
make sounds. They use **body
language** to **communicate**.

Hunting

Great White Sharks are good hunters. They have good hearing and eyesight. They have a great sense of smell.

14

Great White Sharks catch their meals by swimming upward very fast. They **burst** out of the water to catch their **prey**.

Food

A great white shark's favorite meals are sea lions and seals.

Baby Great White Sharks

Baby great white sharks are called **pups**. Pups live on their own after they are born.

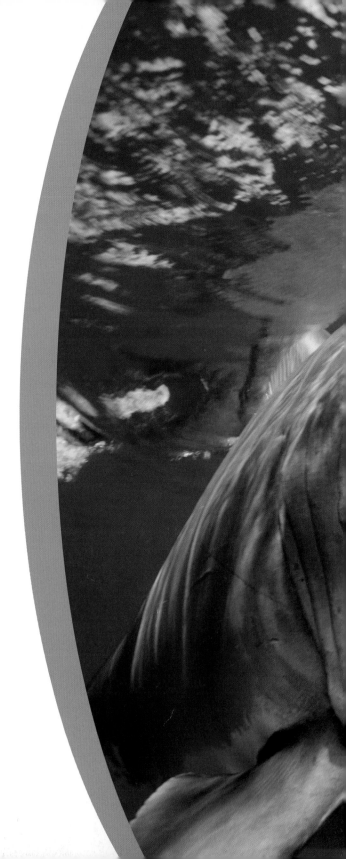

21

More Facts

- Young great white sharks usually do not survive their first year of life.

- After a big meal, great white sharks can go about one to two months without eating.

- A great white's teeth can be more than 2.5 inches (6.35 cm) long.

- Great whites can roll their eyes back into their heads. This is to protect their eyes while they're catching **prey**.

Glossary

body language – communicating without words.

burst – to appear suddenly.

communicate – to give and receive information.

mild – moderately warm.

prey – an animal hunted or killed for food.

pup – a newborn animal.

Index

abdokids.com

Use this code to log on to abdokids.com and access crafts, games, videos and more!

Abdo Kids Code:
SGK0656

DATE DUE

SEP 2 8 2017			
			PRINTED IN U.S.A